AF317030

The Trifecta of Willie Lynch Curse and Our Return to the Genesis

The Trifecta of Willie Lynch Curse and Our Return to the Genesis

A Letter to the African Male and Female and Leadership Amongst African Men

Yahmeen Ben Israel

Contents

First and Foremost...

I would like to give all honor and praises to the Most Holy, to the God of our fathers, the God of Abraham, Isaac, and Jacob; the God of the Genesis Creation, who remembered the covenant that was made with our fathers and did not leave us in the land of captivity. The God who has delivered us out of the iron furnace and allowed us to once again live in that Great and Holy land of ours.

I would also like to give a special dedication to Ben Ammi, who, through a trying time, answered the call to journey back to the Holy Land and restore truth back to the Adamic Civilization. And to all of the elders who bravely withstood the impossible; without you, these words would not exist.

A great appreciation for my publication team, Naara and Daniela. I am grateful and thankful.

To Storm Jordan's Media, I am also thankful.

Last but not least, to my sons, Messiah and Jeremiah, whose faces continue to inspire and challenge me as a Man and Father. I love you, my sons.

Introduction

Throughout the centuries, the Bible has done more than just inspire the physical realm; it has shaped the very essence of man. Truth cannot be told as the word of God stands in absence, and one cannot fully grasp and make the necessary changes by reading the Bible from the middle and onward. The masters of deception have led the Adamic civilization into an abyss, and unless Truth becomes their new master, there is no possible way out of their current predicament.

The purpose of this writing serves as an urgency in the reeducating, reimagining, and redefining of words and characters shaped by an evil doctrine. In this enslaved state, a word/doctrine was forcefully placed upon a people in order to induce fear, reinforce control, and for the "good" of the economy.

The Spirit of Err has made numerous successful attempts to use the African woman against the African man as early as the beginning of Genesis, which we will touch on in this work. This cowardly individual has always been afraid of the man God created in His image and formed from the soil of the earth by making attempts through his woman. As they had fallen away from the instructions and protection of the Creator, Adam (Man) and Eve (Woman) became prey and a conspiracy to the very insidious mind God instructed a forewarning of.

Through higher education, the Spirit of Err, or Satan, has convinced the Adamic civilization that such can be obtained without God being at the center. The mind, in the institutions of the Euro-gentile, is described as something that thinks, remembers, imagines and is capable of reasoning. However, with all of these many definitions, these great scholars could never relate the mind to the primordial stage of death according to the Genesis creation. Higher education, under the Euro-gentile, puts death in its first stage, as the traditional burial, tying into with the Power to Define.

The Power to Define in the hands of the wicked is a weapon of oppression and a satanic control method. It goes beyond thought and challenge. Terms such as thugs, rich, poor, higher education, etc, are all connected to the Power to Define.

Affecting the lives of millions of Africans through the use of words and education, the ramifications that follow are still evident in the present plight of Africans globally. An achievement so perfect that it could only be authorized by God and planned meticulously by men of evil intent.

Today, in this preeminent moment of time, the Africans in America must take the divine charge to Subdue and have dominion over the earth once again. For the sake of our future on this planet depends upon regaining access to the Tree of Life. We must once again hold fast to the divine perception: "When you see me, you shall see my Father." We must be reminded of the conversation between Nicodemus that compelled Jesus to inform him of the essential need to be "born again." With all of Nicodemus's achievements, his credentials did not allow him the title of a "living soul." **(John 3:1-21)**.

As we begin to expose how the word "submit" was weaponized in playing a major role in the possession of our souls, the breaking process of the African woman, the destruction of the Black man's image, and children raised in reversed roles, we must accept the reality that it's all or nothing, life or death. Restoring the use of divine words back to the African family, the whole function of man, woman, and child is interdependent; one cannot survive without the other.

"Emancipate from mental slavery; none but ourselves can free our minds." Commonly associated with Bob Marley, it actually originated with Marcus Garvey.

About the Author

Yahmeen Ben Israel, born Jerrin Grissom, was born at Bethesda North Hospital in Cincinnati, Ohio, to Alice Grissom. A devoted father to two boys. Yahmeen faced the harrowing reality of being behind bars for most of his high school days. Yet, nothing could extinguish his spirit. After reclaiming his freedom in his senior year, he graduated from Hughes Center in Cincinnati. However, mere weeks post-graduation, on June 3, 2009, he confronted a life-threatening encounter when he was shot. A month later, he ventured to California with his cousin, chasing dreams of college football at Golden West College.

Following a failed enlistment in the United States Army, Yahmeen reconnected with a neighborhood friend who unveiled his true identity as a Hebrew Israelite. Committed to a journey of Truth, he devoted himself to educating others about the authentic legacy of Africans in America.

Embracing a vegan lifestyle for over a decade, Yahmeen also lived in Atlanta, Ga, where he developed a keen sense of culture and spirituality

After returning from Israel in 2015, Yahmeen completed his carpentry training in the same year. While attending Cincinnati State, he connected with like-minded brothers, culminating in the momentous Million Man March. In 2018,

Yahmeen obtained his CDL, working first as a school bus driver and then as a Greyhound driver.

After life's misfortunes, and at the time of this writing, Yahmeen found himself homeless. With God in his heart and the spirit of courage and determination, Yahmeen would also found New Species LLC, promoting truth, veganism, and Israelite culture among Africans in the Diaspora.

Notes to Our Reader

You will frequently encounter the use of the term "Euro-gentile" throughout this work. It is a term coined by the African Hebrew Israelites in keeping with our having seized the "Power to Define," a concept that was discussed in detail in the book God the Black Man and Truth.

The suffix "gentile" simply denotes a people or nation that is without the knowledge of the True and Living God of Creation. When using the term "Euro-gentile" (often interchangeably with "Euro-American"), we are, in fact, referring to the entire European family of nations, i.e., Europe, the United States of America, Canada, New Zealand, Australia, etc.

Its usage also reflects the persuasive and powerful social, economic, cultural, and political influence these nations have wielded on this planet. As such, though, these "Euro-gentile" nations are obviously and unquestionably responsible for having brought all of humanity and creation to the brink of destruction as a result of their continuously evil activities and deeds. No racist or otherwise negative connotations are inferred from the phrase.

You will also notice the capitalization of the word "Black" when referring to race, as opposed to merely color. We are well aware that this usage may not conform to generally accepted norms of the English language.

While the use of "Black" may thus be deemed inaccurate, it must be recognized that many "Blacks" or "Africans" have not yet arrived at the point of tracing and identifying their particular nation of origin or nationality. It is an obvious fact that our skins are black and that "Black Americans" hail collectively from the continent of Africa.

The true name of the Creator, **Yahwah (יהוה)** **(YHWH)** or **Yah (יה),** which reflects His Eternal Oneness, has been deliberately removed from usage in the Bible. Thus, it has been replaced by the term God- a more modern and generally accepted term among most religions. More often than not, in assuming "God" is whatever or whoever is intended, there is no direct understanding of our connection to the Ancient Biblical heritage.

Most significantly, "Yah" or "YAH-HO-WAH" identifies the God of the Genesis Creation, the Almighty God, the true God of the Bible: the spiritual force representing righteousness, love, peace, and all things positive and good. You are to see Yah in those who are made in his image or likeness **(John 14:9)**, a verse deceptively used to fit Christian doctrine.

The Tree of Knowledge of Good and Evil refers to an individual and their actions. This tree was considered to be the most shrewd of all the beasts of the field. With spiritual discernment, one can recognize this tree by the fruit it bears or the actions thereof **(Matthew 7:16-20)**.

Jacob, whose name was changed to Israel (**Genesis 32:26-29**), had 12 sons who became the Children of Israel and God's firstborn (**Exodus 4:22**). The Hebrews, or the children of Israel, were given the divine charge to be the light and salt of the earth (**Matthew 5:13-14**) to correct the social, political, and spiritual behaviors of men.

"And they shall teach my people the difference between the holy and profane."

— Ezekiel 44:23.

"For thou art a holy people unto the Lord thy God; the Lord thy God hath chosen thee to be a special people unto himself, above all people who are upon the face of the earth."

— Deuteronomy 7:6

Daniel Chapter 2:44 symbolizes the signs of the time and the end of the Euro-gentile reign.

"And in the days of those kings shall the God of heaven set up a kingdom, which shall never be destroyed; nor shall the kingdom be left to another people; it shall break in pieces and consume all these kingdoms, but it shall stand forever."

As the African Hebrew Israelites of Jerusalem are now back in Israel, or what is called the "Promised Land" or "Holy Land," marks the subsequent establishment of the Kingdom of God on earth.

Adam represented the seed of Truth, the first and only begotten Son of God (Yah). He was fashioned and formed from the soil of the earth, a place for seeds to be planted and fruit to be yielded. The breath of life breathed into Adam was a definite character and nature, sanctifying him as God's (Yah's) representative on earth.

The Power invested by God (Yah) into the hands of man is known as the Spiritual Magna Carta. This power which had been invested into the hands of our enemies. The Europeans, when accepting the Magna Carta, committed themselves to the use of three persuasions: (1) the persuasion of religion; (2) the persuasion of politics - promising great socio-economic benefits; (3) the persuasion of force - violent suppression of all opposition. That power has now been returned to those anointed and appointed by God (Yah).

Our use of the term "Satan" refers to the spirit or force commonly called "devil" or "Spirit of Err." This negative spirit may possess a person or groups of people, causing them to be in total opposition to God (Yah). Its presence is revealed in the actions, thoughts, and vile character of an individual.

Many other words and terms may be capitalized, e.g., "Truth," "Divine," "Love," and "Power to Define." When they appear in such formal usage, it denotes their application as a principle "building block ' or concept in the New World Order.

* * *

Through deliberate misrepresentation, the Bible has often been presented as merely a religious text rather than embraced and examined as a historical record. Moreover, it is often approached in a way that begins merely from the middle and onward. Who has engaged the masses to read, inarguably, the most profound book studied by scholars in this manner? Certainly, it is those who have perpetuated a legacy of deceit.

The Bible is, in fact, a written account of a people's history: the rebellion, consequence, and ultimately, the redemption of the Children of Israel. The arrival of Africans in America marks the most monumental involuntary migration in human existence. However, this horrific transition was divinely ordained, and only by the same divine intervention can it be rectified. Because the "Children of Israel" deliberately chose to turn away from the path of truth, their current abode is "hell on earth," presently under the dominion of their enemies.

And it shall come to pass, if thou shalt hearken diligently unto the voice of the LORD thy God, to observe to do all His commandments which I command thee this day, that the LORD thy God will set thee on high above all the nations of the earth.

But it shall come to pass, if thou wilt not hearken unto the voice of the LORD thy God, to observe to do all His commandments and His statutes which I command thee this day, that all these curses shall come upon thee and overtake thee.

"And the LORD shall bring thee back into Egypt in ships, by the way whereof I said unto thee: Thou shalt see it no more again, and there ye shall sell yourselves unto your enemies for bondmen and for bondwomen, and no man shall redeem you."

— Deuteronomy 28:1, 15, 68 (Modified)

Chapter 1
To Submit: From the James River, 1712

What comes to mind when you hear the word " Submit?" Documents for a legal matter, business plans, a relationship with God or being under the authority of another? And why does this word appear to be so offensive? Is it because the word "submit" has negative connotations of extreme authority that both men and women find offensive? If this is so, who has the authority to give words its meaning? And where does the seed of such offense derive from? Keep in mind, whoever yields the Power to Define either controls the minds of a people or frees the minds of a people.

This power hones in on two spirits: the spirit of good and the spirit of evil. If the spirit of evil possesses this power, words are then used as a weapon of oppression. In contrast to the spirit of righteousness, whose words are then used to keep a people liberated.

First, let's define the word "**Submit**" from the Merriam-Webster Dictionary:

Transitive verb
1: a- to yield to governance or authority. b- to subject to a condition, treatment, or operation.
2: to present or propose to another for review, consideration, or decision.
3: to put forward an opinion or contention.

In the aforementioned definition, the transitive verb (1b) states that "submit" is subject to a condition, treatment, or operation. Remember, the Power to Define in the hands of the wicked is a weapon of oppression. A weapon is described as something (such as a club, knife, or gun) used to injure, defeat, or destroy.* However, words, too, are known as weapons used to injure, defeat, or destroy. As I begin to bring my point to light, I'm certain that many of the people reading this book are aware of the horrendous conditions and treatments of slavery against African males and females. In fact, none is more traumatized than the Africans in America. The conditions to which the African in America has been subjected can even be associated with absurd titles such as "nigger" and "negro."

If the Power to Define in the hands of the wicked is not used as a weapon of oppression, then how does a word such as "submit" gain its definition? And are these definitions being defined by men of righteousness or men of evil intent? I can assure you the Power to Define in the hands of righteous men will bring forth Godliness, love and peace. Yet, it's just

---

* Merriam-Webster Dictionary

the opposite in the hands of men with malicious intent. Their only purpose is satanic control, using the Spirit of Err as power or authority to rule (Spiritual Magna Carta).

As the slaves were taught how to be slaves, there first had to be an outline of what a slave was; one had to define and then bring forth. Since the Euro-gentiles' objective was to dehumanize the Africans in America, they were steadfast to the idea of "How to Teach a Slave to Be a Slave" or "The Making of a Slave." In an attempt to make a slave, there were countless casualties. You had those who were unwavering, and you had those who were forced to "submit" by death as a cruel way of manipulation, torture, or the "bullwhip," an old slave method used for control. An act so diabolical that it resulted in the Black male and female enemies and competitors of one another.

The Willie Lynch Letter and "The Making of A Slave" were delivered on the banks of the James River on the 25th of December in the year 1712. Put on your examining lenses and take notice of the day and month. Now put on your thinking cap and consider an evil doctrine addressed on how to make a slave, given by and to slave owner(s) on Christmas Day, on the banks of the James River, in credence to King James, the sponsor of the translated English Christian Bible. An achievement so flawless that it could only be sanctioned by God and planned meticulously by men of evil intent.

This letter or doctrine is an execrable illustration of how fear, distrust, and envy were used to control the slaves against one another. An integral part of this fear was called "The Breaking Process of the African Woman". Below I will share an excerpt from this chapter of the book mentioned above.

The Breaking Process of the African Woman

"Take the female and run a series of tests on her to see if she will submit to your desires willingly. Test her in every way because she is the most important factor for good economics. If she shows any sign of resistance in submitting completely to your will, do not hesitate to use the bill whip on her to extract that last bit of resistance out of her."

"Take care not to kill her, for in doing so, you spoil good economics. When in complete submission, she will train her offspring in their early years to submit to labor when they come of age. Understanding is the best thing".

"Therefore, we shall go deeper into this area of the subject matter concerning what we have produced here in this breaking process of the female nigger. We have reversed the relationship in her natural uncivilized state, where she would have a strong dependency on the uncivilized nigger male, and she would have a limited protective tendency toward her independent male offspring and would raise male offspring to be dependent like her".

"Nature has provided for this type of balance. We reversed nature by burning and pulling a civilized nigger apart and bullwhipping the other to the point of death, all in her presence. By her being left alone, unprotected, with the male image destroyed, the ordeal caused her to move from her psychologically dependent state to a frozen, independent state. In this frozen, psychological state of independence, she will raise her male and female offspring in reversed roles."

After the ingestion of such graphic information, one can surmise that the digestion produces the same effect. When we, as a people, initiate the divine charge to redefine these sadistic words, only then can we begin to find solutions in the excretion process. The solution to our male and female relationships, parent and child relationships, leadership among men, and our natural relationship with the Creator is the primary source of the problems that continue to beset us as a people.

Let's take the first paragraph of "The Breaking Process of the African Woman." The slave masters were instructed to run a series of tests on her to see if she would submit to their desires willingly. "If she shows any sign of resistance in submitting completely to your will, do not hesitate to use the bullwhip on her to extract that last bit of resistance out of her."

What's profound about this paragraph is that the mind responsible for this ungodly doctrine still applies these same tactics (tests), using the woman of Genesis as a vehicle against her man and their offspring(s).

In the introduction of this writing, I mentioned how this cowardly individual made numerous successful attempts to use the African Edenic woman of Genesis as a vehicle against Adam.* What did this coward fear by going around the man and through his woman as a means to subdue them both? He could have simply appeared to the man (Adam), being as daring as he was. Adam was, in fact, the earthly image, likeness, and form of a God on earth.

In the book of Genesis, this spirit starts its "series" of tests on the African woman. He, too, wanted to see if she would submit willingly or put up resistance.

In **Genesis chapter 3, verses 1-6**, it states:

---

* See Notes to the Reader, Adam.

1 Now the serpent was more subtle than any beast of the field which the LORD God had made. And he said unto the woman, Yea, hath God said: Ye shall not eat of any tree of the garden? 2 And the woman said unto the serpent, 'Of the fruit of the trees of the garden, we may eat.' 3 But of the fruit of the tree which is in the midst of the garden, God hath said: 'Ye shall not eat of it, neither shall ye touch it, lest ye die. 4 And the serpent said unto the woman: 'Ye shall not surely die; 5 For God doth know that in the day ye eat thereof, then your eyes shall be opened, and ye shall be as God, knowing good and evil. 6 And when the woman saw that the tree was good for food and that it was a delight to the eyes, and that the tree was to be desired to make one wise, she took of the fruit thereof, and did eat; and she also gave unto her husband with her, and he did eat."

Here, a question is posed to elicit a response from her to see if she would give the correct answer. 'Yea, have God said: "Ye shall not eat of any tree of the garden?" If we remove the substance of the question, we also find another point to be made.

Prior to this run-in, there was no indication that this ungodly individual had known if she had been taught properly or not. (Read Genesis chapters 1 and 2.) He simply asked, "Yea, hath God said: Ye shall not eat of any tree of the garden?"

Not only was this a test to see if she would submit

willingly, but rather to see if she would use any resistance or had been listening.

As we move into verses 2 and 3, we can clearly see in her response that she most certainly was taught by Adam; the instructions were given to him (see Genesis 2:16-17).

So what happened? She either wasn't taught right, she hadn't been listening to what she had been taught, or, as it is described:

> the serpent was more subtle than any beast of the field".

Now, in verse 4, he begins to make his move against the woman; he reveals himself by saying,

> For God doth know that in the day ye eat thereof, then your eyes shall be opened, and ye shall be as God, knowing good and evil."

Because she hadn't been listening to what she was taught, it didn't require much resistance at all. In fact, it was a willful submission that continues to cause her and her man turmoil.

> And she also gave unto her husband with her, and he did eat."

Following the derivation of this coward from Genesis, it's obvious that his ruse remains the same. He never attempts to displace the African man head-on; instead, the displacement comes at the hands of his woman, as they have become obvious enemies of one another.

I'd like to point out a statement made by Willie Lynch as

he boastfully shares the results of his experiment on the African woman to those like-minded. He said, "Understanding is best". What did he mean by such a statement? Was he insisting that they grasp what he was saying? Possibly, but I can assure you this statement has a much more in-depth meaning. Let's again extract a definition from the Merriam-Webster Dictionary of the word understanding.

Understanding: 2(b): The power to make experience intelligible by applying concepts and categories.

We know power is having authority over something or someone. Now, it becomes the power or authority to make an experience intelligible (capable of being understood) by applying (forceful) concepts (ideas) and categories (of having particular shared characteristics of African women).

Before we arrive at this conclusion, let's continue analyzing the finished product of "The Breaking Process of the African Woman."

Proudly speaking of his previous results of atrocities in the West Indies, he went on to note, "Take care not to kill her, for in doing so, you spoil good economics. When in complete submission, she will train her offsprings in early years to submit to labor when they become of age". To keep someone in complete submission requires one to have quite the obedience. To submit indicates a person's will is involved, which is very important in regard to the development of their character.

As she was forced to witness inhumane methods against the African male, it became entirely a part of such statements as "Understanding is best" or "to get her to understand is best." In other words, she is to be and remain in complete submission to the authority of a lesser man through an experience capable of being understood as a result of a forceful idea(s). He made it clear they did not want to kill her, but instead, they did that which instills fear, and this became the substance of "Understanding is best". As a result of this inhumane approach by methods used as a means to submit, the mental and moral qualities of the Africans in America lack these developments in their character.

Consider this: a civilized "nigger" is said to be one who is polite and well-mannered. That would imply an uncivilized "nigger" is just the opposite. When a man goes to commit a crime and now has to face the consequences of his actions, one might say he deserves it and doesn't think much about it. However, when a man has to face similar consequences for his innocence, a feeling of sympathy kicks in, but no one really goes to the extent of causing an uproar. Fear in the subconscious develops, hoping that you'll never have to experience such a day. This developed into the same fear in the consciousness of the African woman for her male offspring.

Deliberately being given a front-row seat to the burning and tearing apart of a "civilized nigger" who nearly gets beaten to death, the statement "Understanding is best" has officially taken effect.

When the killing or burning of a "civilized nigger," one who carries himself appropriately, is equivalent to the punishment of an uncivilized nigger, something psychological occurs. The fear of always protecting her male offspring rests permanently in the subconscious of the African woman. By being left alone, unprotected, and with the male image destroyed, the ordeal causes her to move from her psychologically dependent state to a frozen, independent state. In her subconscious, she'll never forget the "civilized nigger," for such tragedy doesn't require a delayed effect of fear; the effect sets in immediately. As a result, she raises her male offspring to be physically strong but mentally weak (dependent); she's his example of a protector.

Another aspect of raising him to ensure his safety is that she teaches him how to also submit to a lesser man. To keep his head down, she wishes he does not end up like the civilized nigger. The problem, in addition to that, is that being reduced to what is called a "nigger" is beyond words; it's an action, a deadly one in many cases. Once a man ends up being stripped of his manhood, what's left? In order for a male to grow into a man, his manhood must remain intact. It's actually like a double-edged sword, with both sides being negative; on one side, he'll never be the protector his family needs him to be, and on the other, he'll never develop into what is called a "man." That is not to say he will never grow. If a male becomes an adult but never becomes a man, then those dependent on him (woman, child) will also face a lack of development.

Never in antiquity has the African woman ever heard such a term as "Head of the family."

"The Breaking Process of the African Woman" attests that such a term didn't exist prior to her enslavement. The term came forth from this frozen, psychological state of independence. Please give heed; these weren't just slave owners and/or friends; they were conspirators conspiring to destroy a nation of African people. Once a thought or idea is conceived in the mind and then birthed, the finished product is a result of that mind or idea. Unfortunately, the frozen, psychological state of independence embedded in the

African woman is a finished product of the mind/idea of an evil conspiracy. Unless divine intervention occurs, there is no possible way out of her frozen state.

Take a young woman who is a product of an independent mother. She watches her mother work, labor, and toil day after day. The mother also assumes the role of a protector not only for her daughter but for her son as well. She is being trained to uphold the same frozen, psychological state of independence, a role she's been illegitimately thrust into by men of evil intent.

Before an actor or actress could assume a role in a movie, they first had to practice and be qualified. But who qualifies for their role? Certainly not the actors or actresses themselves. A casting team, including the casting director, determines who is qualified or not. It doesn't take an individual with a master's degree to conclude that the African woman in America, nor her female offspring, were ever qualified to play the role of a man. The casting team and the casting director deliberately set them up for mere destruction. She was purposely groomed to carry the load of what was originally a coalition between man and woman.

This unimaginable psychological damage doesn't come without results. The epoch of slavery set the Africans in America on a course of complete chaos and destruction, hoping they would never regain their consciousness.

Good economics referred to her reproductive capabilities, bearing children who would also become enslaved. The burdens, both physical and psychological, that came with childbearing were enormous for enslaved women. Expected to put the needs of the master and his family before her own children, she would return to the fields soon after giving birth, leaving her child to be raised by others and grappling with the additional responsibilities that were added on top of her usual duties. For the love of their children, slave mothers often chose to stay in bondage while their male counterparts attempted to escape. The female slave was, moreover, faced with the prospect of being forced into sexual relationships for the purposes of reproduction, tormented by the haunting thought that one day her female offspring could suffer the same torment.

It's an old saying that says, "There is nothing new under the sun". In this case, "there is nothing new under the control of the Euro gentile". If we translate this into today's society, it's evident that the Black woman still suffers the same fate of childbearing. She is constantly expected to put the needs of her master or employer ahead of her own child, having someone else raise the children. On many jobs, she is not given the adequate amount of time to give birth, heal, and learn about her child. Not soon after she gives birth, her return to the plantation (job) is imminent; bills have it's way of coming like clockwork.

The psychological wounds run deep within the soul, intricately woven within the conscious and subconscious fabric of the Africans in America. Every facet of their lives since arriving on the shores of Virginia is a direct result of a cunning and relentless scheme orchestrated by the Euro-gentiles, a plot designed with treachery to dismantle and erase the spirit of the identity of the Africans in America.

Take into account the brute force it would have taken to strip the African male of his manhood and the forceful methods used in the breaking process of the African woman. Would a run for freedom be an option on the table for them both? In most cases, the African male would attempt to make a daring escape by himself, leaving his woman and children vulnerable to the dangers already presented to them. However, it was the decision of the African woman to keep her and her offspring in bondage out of fear for their lives.

Still holding on to what's left of his manhood, it's an option that doesn't guarantee much freedom, but death surely has its place.

It has been said, There are four possible ways that a victim of a system can respond: they can submit, they can cooperate, they can resist, or they can engage in destruction. But I say, Or they can return to the will and plan of God and subdue and have dominion as it is written.

A return cannot begin until we start the process of re-educating and redefining words rooted in deception. With there being a possession of the African soul, there must be a repossessing. A clear assessment of the issue can be made only when people truly desire freedom. This should stand as a singular aspiration, for their survival on this planet dictates it.

Chapter 2
A Letter to the African Man

Then the LORD God formed man of the dust
of the ground and breathed into his nostrils the
breath of life, and man became a living soul."

— Genesis 2:7

What happened to the Soul brother or African male of the
Genesis creation? Clearly, he's not the same man following
his arrival to the colony of Virginia. How did he lose his salt
(flavor) to season the earth and its inhabitants? How did his
reputation become that of a drunkard, drugged, bad husband,
bad father, non-protector, uneducated, lazy, treacherous, and
dishonest, to name the least? Who gave him such a
reputation, or is he solely responsible? As we expose the
reputation of the African male in America and his fragile
relationship with his woman, he must bravely face the
psychological damage done to himself by his oppressor. He
must acknowledge that he, too, played a role in his downstate.

No longer can the Euro-gentile be considered a stumbling block for the African male, for the return of the Genesis man (Adam) is long overdue.

Going back to the **2nd chapter of Genesis, verses 16-17,** man receives his instructions from the Creator.

> 16 And the LORD God commanded the man, saying: 'Of every tree of the garden thou mayest freely eat"; 17 But of the tree of the knowledge of good and evil, thou shalt not eat of it; for in the day that thou eatest thereof, thou shalt surely die."

First and foremost, the instructions were given to man; this was a sign of God establishing order, and the instructions were clear. Man, in return, repeated this same order and taught his woman, but neither did he nor she give an ear.

> And the woman said unto the serpent: 'Of the fruit of the trees of the garden we may eat; "but of the fruit of the tree which is in the midst of the garden, God hath said: Ye shall not eat of it, neither shall ye touch it, lest ye die.'"

> — Genesis 3: 2-3

As we approach the fall of man at the hands of his woman, the African male must be aware of two dangers. One which comes through an opposing doctrine in opposition to God and the other at the very source of his being, his woman. Since her creation, she's had quite an independent mind.

Roaming freely, doing as she pleases, causing her man to suffer with her. But man hasn't been quite the leader, instead the opposite, following behind his woman. In the verse below, man clearly abandons the order of creation, moving from the head to the tail.

> And when the woman saw that the tree was good for food and that it was a delight to the eyes, and that the tree was to be desired to make one wise, she took of the fruit thereof and did eat; and she also gave unto her husband with her, and he did eat"
>
> — Genesis 3:6

What's clear is the African male has been failing since Genesis. Failing to listen and failing to apply the proper knowledge. Carrying out the complete opposite as instructed not to do. Instructions that were given to protect his life and health. Man was simply undisciplined and he allowed his woman to lead him astray. He failed to recall the establishment of order and his purpose. Beyond that, he should have recognized the woman of Genesis was not the same woman God created, a helpmate. What changed? Was it her physical that looked different? In fact, the way she spoke, she ate of (listened to, and accepted a different truth) the tree of knowledge of good and evil. It should have sounded strange to him but he was not himself either. A lesson the African man must learn in this is to take a woman of the Genesis creation, a woman of him, a helpmate.

Being unsuccessful in protecting his woman, he couldn't even protect himself. Sure, she ate of (listened to) and has been held responsible. Now, when she first came to him, he should have rejected her and asked, "Who have you been listening to?" He even hid himself from the presence of God along with his woman.

> And they heard the voice of the LORD God walking in the garden toward the cool of the day, and the man and his wife hid themselves from the presence of the LORD God among the trees of the garden."
>
> — Genesis 3:8

Till this very day, the African male struggles to face the same reality of Genesis. He continues to hide himself from the presence of his Maker (his father), fearful and ashamed. He has yet to learn that his ears are his greatest organs and that the instructions given were as a light for his soul. God spoke, but he did not listen; however, for him, this is a clear solution to his troubles and likewise hers.

The African male cannot continue to be the "nigger," "negro," and "nigga" of America's history. He is so psychologically damaged that he, too, refers to himself and his brethren in the same demeaning language, deceiving himself by using it as a term of endearment and, with the same tongue, as a weapon before destruction, identical to his oppressor.

He has been taught to hate his colored skin, his countenance, his woman, his child, his brethren, his mind, and, most importantly, his God. In exchange for the God of his captors, what a brain surgical procedure! The only praise he receives is if he is an entertainer of some sort and exemplifies a charitable spirit toward what I would call a debatable cause. With all the money he is being paid, he feels loved, appreciated, and respected. In contrast, no respect is given to him for being a father to his children, a protector and provider of the home, the strength of the family, the builder of civilization, and the creator of the many inventions known to man. Who deprives him of being acknowledged for such credits but purposely ruins his image? The African male surely does not control his own history, let alone his own destiny.

What can the African male in America be proud of? A big house, fancy vehicles, nice clothes, jewelry, sleeping with numerous women, or having a lot of money? Should he not be ashamed that he has no manhood, his woman doesn't respect him, and his children don't honor him? He has no culture and no language of his own; neither can he protect nor provide properly for his family. To say the least, his brain is severely scrambled. He takes joy in having nothing of his own, constantly celebrating a life of destruction in the lands of his enemy. He's the most incarcerated and hated race in what he calls "his country," yet he has the most to celebrate.

We've learned through the harrowing accounts detailed in "The Willie Lynch" letter the dreadful torment the Black male suffered, being burned and nearly beaten to death all in front of his woman and possibly children. We also addressed the Black woman too suffered the same fate. With the use of deadly fear and without protection, guidance, discipline, and stability, she fell victim to a trap laid meticulously for her. The horrific crimes sought by her eyes, in fear for her offspring, caused the Black woman to submit and remain subdued to the Euro gentile. Constant rape, physical abuse, and a lingering fear of her female offspring enduring a similar fate and always in fear of the life of her male offspring. She's been overwhelmingly taking on the majority of the load, raising children by herself, feeding, clothing, providing shelter, protection, finances, and schooling, while having no time to heal herself. Indeed, a position self-inflicted as well as a participation unwillingly.

Significantly influenced by European doctrine, she ascended beyond the Black male, insisting on becoming "Head of the Family," a ranking status given to her by her "new man," the Euro gentile. Her new identity became that of his woman, "the European woman." Anytime a woman is fighting for the attention of another woman's man, she will always find a need to rally for the same pleasures he gives his woman.

Let's take the 1st of the 4 waves of the feminist movement starting in the mid-1800s, the first organized movement aimed at gaining rights for "American women" in Seneca Falls, New York. These were the Rights of equality and the right to vote. Because the 15th Amendment gave all men the right to vote, it angered European women that African men were being granted suffrage before her. This ultimately led to the Women's suffrage movement" - a decades-long fight to win the right to vote for women in the United States. Unlike European women's right to vote, African women faced continuous obstacles.

A crucial question needs to be asked here: Who were Black women truly voting for? The Black man? Or perhaps the same man accountable for raping, maiming, murdering, destroying, and creating turmoil for her and her family? She's undoubtedly trapped in Genesis, eyeing and desiring what she considers pleasant. She's the exemplary case of eyes that cannot see.

A book published by Betty Friedan called "The Feminine Mystique" launched the wave of the second feminist movement in 1963. She argued that women were chafing against the confines of their roles as wives and mothers. She explored the idea of women finding personal fulfillment outside of their traditional roles. Similar to the suffrage movement, second-wave feminism received backlash, concentrating only on privileged European women. In response, Black women decided to form their own feminist movements. Including the National Black Feminist Organization (NBFO).

In all truth, the African woman has intended to impersonate the European woman at every turn. Feeling marginalized, the second feminist movement was inspired by the civil rights movement, with the African male and female standing hand in hand. The demonstration of large-scale activism and nonviolent protest tactics led European women to believe they could fight for equality through similar methods and political strategies.

1990s feminism encouraged women to express their sexuality and individuality; this was considered the third wave of the feminist movement, a movement also popularized by African women. Each and every one of these movements or organizations was formed by European women and additionally advanced at the hands of Black women.

With the fourth movement being almost the same as the third, many find it difficult to define, but I define it as the "Reversed Roles" Movement. It's obvious many women, in particular, have managed to consume the identity of the male species in general. Relating to the affairs of Black men and women in America, she certainly consumed his identity, every bit of it, and he, too, hers. With his ungodly acts of homosexuality and dress-wearing, he has become the Euro gentiles' creation of the Black man in America, or African American. While she's paying all the bills, wearing the pants, calling all the shots, and being compensated for "Head of the Family," she too is the Euro gentiles' creation of the Black woman.

She allows him the luxury of lounging at home, playing video games, changing diapers, being unable to hold a job, creating entrepreneurship for his family, and hanging out with his other visionless friends while she sustains them both. The Black woman has become more masculine than the Black man in America. Just as the Black man has become more European than the European and more feminine than his Black counterpart.

In the chapter "Letter to the African Woman," an attempt is made to release her of all charges brought against her by her man. Although valid accusations exist, they are moot until he embraces his rightful position; he must ensure that he strengthens his foundation first. This doesn't imply she's exempt from his judgment; that has been the very barrier between them. She's been deceptively granted too much freedom and power of separation. What it does imply is him setting a righteous standard to be mirrored if he has to cast a righteous judgment. I firmly believe that if the Black man gives his woman a new man to desire, he could unthaw her entrenched, frozen psychological state of independence. Faced with a daunting challenge, it's one he must succeed in if he's ever to have a harmonious bond with his woman, children, and Maker.

His role as Godhead should illuminate through his deeds —providing, protecting, and supplying his family with stability, discipline, and love. Understanding the weight of this responsibility, the Black woman becomes an essential partner in this reunion.

What amount of the psychological damage done to the Black woman is at the expense of her man, lacking the ability to lead? Is he the one responsible for her participation in the feminine movements since the mid-1800s? How about the welfare system? Supplying her with every means she needs to live without him, except a father for her children. Should he be accused of her lesbianism, the same movement she willingly participated in, led by European women? She's even tossed aside the "traditional role" of a mother and wife.

Although her price tag comes at its own expense, his price tag is just as hefty. With the inability to free his mind from his dependent state, she will always remain enslaved in her frozen, psychological state of independence. The established order is that a man must always provide the head.

It was not always that he was unable to gain employment to provide; in some aspects, he didn't want to provide. Since the welfare system would do the support, being a man to his woman and a father to his children was least prioritized. Undoubtedly, the welfare system served as a cause and effect, intentionally forcing the Black male from his home into the streets, where he turned to crime and drugs. It was almost like a law: should a man or his belongings be caught in the home when the social worker visited, the woman could be cut from her benefits, a conspiracy the black woman participated in (willingly or unwillingly).

Not having a man and father for her children was the least prioritized as well. Dealing with the pressures of taking care of children in addition to a man was extremely overwhelming in her mind. Being a witness to her mother and her mother's mother carrying the load all by themselves, she, too, feels that she can do it. What she thinks is just a challenge turns out to be a disaster as we bear witness to the mentality and morality of the new generation.

Shahrazad Ali said, "Feeding, clothing, and sheltering a child is called maintaining one. To raise a child requires a parental coalition between a mother and a father". I couldn't agree more, and even so, the majority of Africans in America, truthfully, are well aware of the magnitude of a parental coalition.

The question now becomes, if the Black man can assume his role again, would his woman allow the adversary to continue to use her against her man? There has to be a prerequisite if the African woman in America is to face or challenge this adversarial force. She must bear witness to her man, once again, accepting his role as Godhead. She must see it as a badge of honor, as it very much puts her in the spotlight, indeed. It will test her to see if she has been a willing participant all along or if the African male truly failed to protect and provide for her in some instances.

Just as brain surgery was performed on the African man and woman, they must commit themselves to what was considered a forewarning: "In the day that thou eatest thereof, thou shalt surely die."In order to reverse this death sentence, they participated in (willingly or unwillingly) a rewiring of the mind is imperative. As the Greater Laws (laws given by God to protect man) became supplanted by the lesser laws (laws given by man to man), life became associated with movement, and death became associated with the traditional burial. Christian doctrine has devoured their African souls. European culture has dominated their African culture. They can no longer relate to their African roots. The language of their oppressor has ruled their tongue of speech.

The male offspring, who was shielded and protected by his mother, is more frail than ever. Trapped behind 400 years of mental and physical abuse, he has become the enemy of his own mind, imprisoned by the belief that his state of mind is irreversible. Comfortable with the fact that his woman is calling the shots, making the money, and paying all of the household bills, what an adult male!

Man's solution to his morbid state of mind is a simple return and application to the tree of knowledge or the tree of life. If the proof of eating from the Tree of Knowledge of good and evil is visible in his current state, would not a return offer compelling proof that the instructions given by God were for his survival? Instead, his role is downsized; he is prey to every nation; even the woman of his household rules over him.

She has ventured off into a strange world, influenced by a strange doctrine, having found new love with a strange man. The Black man must not make an all-out attempt to save his woman; it could result in destruction for himself. He must first save himself, restore his soul, and renew his strength. His keen awareness must not fail him again. Only in this form can the Black man introduce to his woman a new man. Only then can he recognize and ask, Who have you been listening to? And convey, "Get away from me, woman." One example where he can and should use this phrase is when his woman is chafing against the confines of her role as a wife and mother. Allow me to articulate this point with the utmost clarity: a woman is well within her right to chase her dreams and to make use of her talents and strengths. However, the duties of her profession should not encroach upon the critical responsibilities she holds as a wife and mother. When her professional duties overshadow these essential roles, it causes disruption within the balance forged in the home. The unity of the household must always remain the foremost priority for both Black men and women. After all, the home is a sanctuary and nurturing ground where love and support must prevail above all else.

Chapter 3
A Letter to the African Woman

22 And the rib, which the LORD God had taken from the man, made He a woman and brought her unto the man. 23 And the man said: 'This is now bone of my bones and flesh of my flesh;"

— Genesis 2:22-23

Where is the African woman (Eve) of the Genesis creation, fashioned and formed by God and declared by man, "bone of my bones, flesh of my flesh?" How did she become so comfortable in a world under evil men whose only intentions are to destroy the very source of her existence? She is none other than a participant (willingly or unwillingly) of an evil doctrine. If she's ever to undo the death sentence that was bestowed upon her, "in the day thou eatest thereof, thou shalt surely die." She must wholeheartedly admit that such a crime (sin) was committed. Once acknowledged and a vow is made, then the process of redemption can be set in motion. She must again allow herself to be formed and fashioned by the hands (words) of God and brought to her man, where he would declare, This is now bone of my bones and flesh of my flesh.

Nowhere in the Genesis narrative can the African woman in America find the "independent woman" she was fashioned to embody, crafted by an ungodly idea. The Spirit of Err, or Satan, is greatly aware of the established order and role of dependency in the Genesis account.

> 'It is not good that the man should be alone; I will make him a help meet for him.'"
>
> — Genesis 2:18

With supreme wisdom, God begins the process of bringing forth a "helpmate" into existence, as a rib (energy) is extracted from man.

Formed from the omnipotent mind of God came a perfect female counterpart, not the "independent" woman of slavery.

From the aforementioned verse, notice that the woman who was created for man was modeled to be a helpmate first, not a wife. Remember, Jesus said, "It is the spirit that quickeneth; the flesh profiteth nothing."

She was the helper of man, his other pair of hands. She takes on what's called the extra load. A helper serves and does whatever she can to make things work smoothly. Take, for example, the First Lady, a preacher's wife, or even the spouse of a farmer. What do each of these women have in common? Are they not cognizant of their duty as a helpmate? Does the First Lady have a more significant role outside of the

Whitehouse needs? Does The Preacher's wife carry outside responsibilities bigger than the church? How about the farmer's wife? Is she seen playing another role beyond the farm, such as a school teacher or some sort?

In many cases, absolutely not, she keeps her hand in the hand of her man. She's what's defined as a member of the "stream room" crew. A man has to always take a woman who is a part of him; Genesis instructs us so.

We can deduce that these women were obviously not deceived. If so, they wouldn't be able to properly fulfill their role as a helpmate. Either they didn't undergo the soul transformation of a slave, or someone sewed in her the importance of the male and female relationship. It seems as if every race of women on this planet understands her role as a helpmate except the African woman in America. Why is this? Does the Black woman naturally lack the ability to perform such a role? Does the Black man naturally lack the ability to protect and provide? Both were considered experiments in the soul transformation of a slave. No other people on the planet have endured physical and more drastic mental change than the African family. Brain surgery was literally performed on the man and his woman in the absence of a hospital or operating table. A procedure not only done by a surgical genius but one that did not require the use of surgical instruments.

The plot to destroy the male image was heavily douced in deception. His images of manhood, fatherhood, husbandhood, and most importantly, his God-image. Take the article from The Washington Post, 26th of February, 2010, by DeNeen Brown, "**Looking Outside the Race Box".** "More single black women being urged to give interracial dating a try".

I extracted a few quotes from the article above to shed light on why the Black male image has been systematically and intentionally destroyed.

"Single black women with college degrees outnumber single black men with college degrees almost 3 to 1 in major urban areas such as Washington, according to a 2008 population survey by the U.S. Census Bureau. Given those numbers, any economist would advise them to start looking elsewhere."

"Black women are in market failure," says writer Karyn Langhorne Folan. "The solution is to find a new market for your commodity. And in this case, we are the commodity, and the new market is men of other races."

"Consider your options, she says. Expand your horizons. Stop listening to your girlfriends. Forget about the brothers calling you a sellout. Get over those old images of slavery and stop blaming every white man for sins perpetrated by others," says Karyn Langhorne Folan, an African female.

The harsh reality that the African woman in America must face is that she was a pawn, strategically used in a satanic way to aid against the destruction of her man. She was literally propelled to believe the Black man God had created for her wasn't the man he (Euro-America) had created for her. He, being a lesser man, deceptively extolled himself above the African male and slithered his way in. An article like this wasn't just haphazardly published, it was stamped on the front cover of the Washington Post, written "urgency" that African women transition into interracial dating.

Let's uncover some facts, exploiting this urgency.

Consider the impactful damages drugs have had on the Black community. There's an alarming amount of evidence to support a conspiracy to destroy the Africans in America, specifically the African males. Take President Richard Nixon, who popularized a term called "War on Drugs" in the year 1971. He declared drug abuse public enemy number one. "In order to fight and defeat this enemy, it is necessary to wage a new, all-out, worldwide offensive," he stated.

Following such a statement, it isn't a coincidence that the incarceration rate of African males dramatically increased, or is it? Even when considering crime rates, the "War on Drugs" significantly led to a sharp rise in incarceration for African males in America, more than for any other racial group. African men became the prominent target.

In fact, 4 years following the 26th of February 2010 article "Looking Outside the Race Box," an article titled **"White people are more likely to deal drugs, but black people are more likely to get arrested for it"** was published on the 30th of September, 2014 by Christopher Ingram.

The purpose of the article was to provide additional proof that the conspiracy to destroy the black male image and remove him from his home is far less than reaching.

The article reads, "Whites were about 45 percent more likely than blacks to sell drugs in 1980, according to an analysis of the National Longitudinal Survey of Youth by economist Robert Fairlie. This was consistent with a 1989 survey of youth in Boston. My own analysis of data from the 2012 National Survey on Drug Use and Health shows that 6.6 percent of white adolescents and young adults (aged 12 to 25) sold drugs, compared to just 5.0 percent of blacks"(a 32 percent difference).

In a 1994 interview with President Nixon's domestic policy chief, John Ehrlichman, after being a public disgrace and having done a stretch in federal prison, he had little left to protect. He said, "You want to know what this was really all about?" He went on:

"The Nixon campaign in 1968, and the Nixon White House after that, had two enemies: the antiwar left and Black people. Do you understand what I'm saying? We knew we couldn't make it illegal to be either against the war or Black, but by getting the public to associate the hippies with marijuana and Blacks with heroin and then criminalizing both heavily, we could disrupt those communities. We could arrest their leaders, raid their homes, break up their meetings, and vilify them night after night on the evening news. Did we know we were lying about the drugs? Of course, we did."

Jobs for the Black male were hard to come by or did not compensate him enough (another ruse in the Euro-gentiles' arsenal). However, drugs were easier to obtain than employment. Not being fully conscious of the plot to destroy him, the Black male decided that if he could not gain employment to provide for his family, then he would appoint himself to a different source of income. A decision that did not turn out well for him or his family. So again, I say, does the Black man naturally lack the ability to protect and provide? It is only because of the provision in his DNA that he has succumbed to this inevitable fate.

Jail and imprisonment started with the African teenage male using narcotics as a means to bring in extra money for his family. One of my oldest brothers was a victim of this conspiracy. He became a father as a 17-year-old teen, living with and providing for his family. In less than a year, he had been employed by numerous companies that always managed to reduce his hours. With bills coming in, he made a decision that would render him a victim of a similar scheme set for hundreds of thousands of other Black males.

Distributing drugs, drug abuse, and crime became the norm in the Black community. The African male in America became an enemy of his own neighborhood, robbing, assaulting, and even murdering his own kind for a high. Having trouble coping with not being able to provide for his family, his dependent state arose. Meeting the consequences of his actions, he now relies on the system to provide his bed, food, and shelter.

As the Black male went to jail, the Black female pursued an education. Welfare for some didn't turn out to be a way forward in her future. But I can assure you, this was not his plan either; he, too, had a divine purpose. With his talents and skillful building, he built America, even in his fallen state. He "sets" the tone in the industries of sports, music, movies, fashion, etc. Even after all of his misfortunes, it is no wonder why he has always been the "target". That's why the article "Black women urged to date outside the race box" is absurd.

After the continuous attempts to destroy and defeat the male image, they suggest the Black woman, due to her college education, "date outside of her race", what a slap in the face. Any Black woman advocating this foolishness needs a real soul-searching. This is not to say love has a color, but due to the inhumane crimes committed against the Black male, the one who committed such offenses suggests his woman move on. That her man is educationally unfit. Who is so bold as to utter this folly? None other than the ungodly snake with a forked tongue.

To educate someone is to develop a person's mind. It is through these ungodly institutions that the Euro-gentile urges the African woman to date outside of her race. She has been fashioned in a world of decadence under a strange idea called "education," mentally, morally, and aesthetically. Take education under the European social system, for instance; it is because of these same institutions of learning that the world is in its current state of turmoil. The air is polluted, the soil is eroded, deforestation, ocean acidification, climate change, etc. The man is weak and lost; his woman and children are off in a world doing strange things, and education has defined these as progress.

Furthermore, is it not the exact institution that developed the minds and morals of the Africans in America through slavery that was deemed legal? Education has nothing to do with advocating for the Black woman to date outside her race. He has another idea in mind, an old and treacherous one, for his thoughts are evil continuously.

Going back to a passage in the "Willie Lynch" letter, I extracted some additional information to bring consciousness back to the Black woman.

In the chapter titled "Warning: Possible Interloping Negatives," Willie Lynch establishes a few definitions for future generations. I have listed one of the definitions below. Keep in mind that these were great conspirators. He grew concerned about the economic plan, purpose, reason, and effect of crossbreeding horses and niggers.

He wrote:

"Crossbreeding niggers means taking so many drops of good white blood and putting them into as many nigger women as possible."

The female slave necessarily dealt with the prospect of being forced into sexual relationships with her captor for the purposes of reproduction.

Remember the article reads, More single black women being urged to give interracial dating a try on the front cover of the Washington Post, one of the leading news organizations in the United States. Who is urging this? One fact we can point out is that whoever is urging this mess is not telling their women to date outside of their race. There's no article urging European women to date African or Black men. It's all used as a weapon of deception: his tricks, tactics, deceptive schemes, and his evil mind. He was more "subtle" than any beast of the field. No longer is he on the plantation sharing his crossbreeding methods with his co-conspirators. He's far more advanced now, causing the African woman to fall into a deeper sleep. He has made his way onto the front cover of the Washington Post, and with her Western education, she has deceitfully been made not to care, or, truthfully, because of her own desires, she may care less.

The Black woman can no longer remain in this frozen, psychological state of independence. It's time to unthaw the brain and regain your higher consciousness. Allow your mind to roam over 300 years ago at the time of this doctrine, when you were forced to submit, causing your frozen, psychological state of independence. On occasions, the master would rape married women, leaving their husbands feeling powerless to protect them. What kind of protection could he provide under his conditions? He was tortured, burned, and murdered for the sake of submission to a lesser man, and he was groomed to be mentally weak by his mother. The incapacity of the Black man to protect his wife from such violation adds to another fundamental aspect of the relationship between Black men and women. The paternalistic language of slavery, the restrictions of slave law, and the circumstances of slave life created a sense of equality between Black wives and husbands.

A slave master's control over both spouses limited the Black man's potential for dominance over his wife.

Needless to forget, the Black woman was an experiment, fashioned and educated in a world strange and hostile to the Black man's very nature. The woman of Genesis was considered a "helpmate"; instead, she has become a "hell mate," indoctrinated into a world in total opposition to the will and plan of God.

I cannot help but think that the Black woman longs to embrace the essence of the woman of Genesis, yearning for the joy that sacred bond once held. Yet, she must not allow the adversary of God to use her again. She must exert that monumental Godly strength like many other women before her. She must equip herself with the proper knowledge of divine nutrition for the betterment of her family.

As a vegan/vegetarian of 12 years, I found in my own personal experiences that it is more difficult to convince a Black woman to pursue a healthier lifestyle than a Black man. In all of her education, she has not learned nor been taught the importance of divine nutrition, which is the act or process of nourishing or being nourished.* Nutrition plays a fundamental role in the growth, reproduction, and survival of the body. This is primarily because her deceptively Western education is disguised as none other than an enslaved indoctrination. Pork, such as the intestines (also called chitlins), salted fish, lard, and vegetables added with ham hock or pig's feet, is still prepared in her kitchen with love. She has been given the ultimate task of killing her husband

---

* Nutrition, Merriam-Webster Dictionary

and their children and taking her along with them. This should serve as evidence that man's ability to live or die has come and is being maintained at the hands of his woman.

She must convince her man that his woman is not the enemy of the home but rather his protection, in a sense, created from his own rib. Just as a rib provides protection to vital organs, she is to safeguard his heart and spirit. Since man was given the mantle of leadership, God fashioned a woman tailored to his needs, created with intention before she could truly serve alongside him.

When a woman is devoid of the proper Godhead, she risks falling victim to four predominant malevolent spirits. Regardless of her financial status, her achievements, her diverse accolades, or the extent of her education, the Black woman remains incomplete until she reunites with her man (her Adam). These spirits manifest as loneliness, depression, gossip, and promiscuity, each vying for control. Yet, she struggles to find an identity while her true identity is entwined with that of her man. In this sacred connection is her true essence.

I urged the African woman to stay within her race, to no longer be fooled by this evil and deceptive spirit. There must be a total commitment in the realignment process of the Genesis creation, to be the "rib" that protects the internal organs of her man.

> God, in giving woman to man, was establishing order. The woman was made the feminine part of men. There was no need for conflict, only understanding. As man was made a God, she was made a female God or Goddess. When a man is made king, she is made queen. When a

man is made prince, she is made princess. Every height, every place, she was always there, for she was him. But God knowing all things, established order to prevent confusion. Authority has always been shared with a woman. God revealed His order because woman had to know that to destroy her man was to destroy herself, for she would lose the source of her being".

— God the Black Man and Truth, p. 51

Chapter 4
Leadership Among African Men

"Come now, let us reason together, saith the Lord."

—Isaiah 1:18

No other prophet makes mention of peace more than the Prophet Isaiah. As the Creator lays bare the continuous sins of the African male (or Children of Israel), an olive branch is extended to the man under the condition that he turn away from his evil and rebellious ways. The same man who unceasingly walks astray as if his predicament is a result of the color of his skin. His drunken state of mind will never allow him to correlate his current plight, his saddening bond with his God, and his brethren. Reasoning does not come without cause and a process of logic. So again, that's what I'm asking: come and reason with me today, brethren; let us relinquish the mind that continues to be housed in chains by an enslaved, ungodly idea. Let us lay bare the multiplicity of issues that prevent the unity of the African male species.

Throughout the course of this disquisition, I have used The Willie Lynch Letter and "The Making of a Slave" as a testament to the systematic subjugation of Africans in America, a plight that erased their identity and threatened their existence. I will say it again and as many times as necessary: these weren't just friends or slave owners; they were conspirators. Evil geniuses plotting to destroy the very fabric of the African soul, man's relationship with his woman, their children, and the camaraderie of brotherhood. Willie Lynch considered his method to be what he coined as a "foolproof"* method. Below, I will give a definition of what a foolproof method is or what it means.

At least two questions must be raised here. How did the Euro gentile get so audacious in his way of thinking? And even more, what were the bases that caused him to become overly confident in his foolproof method? He was sure that if installed correctly, it would control the slaves for a minimum of 300 years, maybe thousands, an evil mind, to say the least.

In search of a solution to their problems with slaves, men from the Colony of Virginia sought to find one man who was maliciously qualified for the position: Willie Lynch. Studying human nature, particularly that of the Black slave, he had prior experience with this so-called foolproof method. In the West Indies, where he experimented with some of the newest and still the oldest methods for slave control, became the basis for his overt confidence and his big ego.

Thoroughly outlining "The Making of a Slave" chapter in the Willie Lynch Letter, a simple little list of differences is given to the slaveholders; it reads:

---

* **Foolproof**: so simple, plain, or reliable as to leave no opportunity for error, misuse, or failure. American Merriam-Webster Dictionary

"On top of my list would be "age" but it's there only because it starts with an "A". The second is "COLOR" or shade, there is intelligence, size, sex, size of plantations and status on plantations, the attitude of owners, whether the slaves live in the valley, on a hill, East, West, North, South, have fine hair, course hair, or is tall or short. Now that you have a list of differences, I shall give you an outline of action, but before that, I shall assure you that distrust is stronger than trust and envy is stronger than adulation, respect, or admiration".

"The black slaves, after receiving this indoctrination, shall carry on and become self-refueling and self-generating for hundreds of years, maybe even thousands. Don't forget you must pitch the old black Male vs. the young black Male and the young black Male vs. the old black Male. You must use the dark skin slaves vs. the light-skinned slaves, and the light-skinned slaves vs. the light-skinned slaves."

"It is necessary that your slaves trust and depend on us. They must love, respect, and trust only us. Gentlemen, these kits are your keys to control. Use them. Have your wives and children use them; never miss an opportunity. If used intensely for one year, the slaves themselves will remain perpetually distrustful of each other".

As I sit back, flipping between local and national news stations, disgusted at the relentless cycle of black-on-black crime, I find myself contemplating the impious methods used on Black male slaves. What's vilified as "thugs" killing each other on the evening news turns out to be something much more underlying. Thugs are merely a misrepresentation of image due to the conspiracy of Black-on-Black violence. This is to say, Black-on-Black crime was factually instituted and sustained through an indoctrination used to conspire. Did they not join together on Christmas Day in the year 1712, on the banks of the James River, to discuss "The Making of a Slave?"

Let's give the definition of **Conspire:** [*]

1. to join in a secret agreement to do an unlawful or wrongful act or an act that becomes unlawful as a result of the secret agreement

2. To act in harmony toward a common end.

Slavery, or the inhumane treatment of Blacks, was very much legal in the Colony of Virginia/America, so it wasn't considered a conspiracy to them, as this ties in with the Power to Define. The secrecy in which the contents of the letter were administered among other co-conspirators signaled a conspiracy, legal or illegal. A conspiracy can only be effective if the victim or victims are led by deception. It was an advantage to intentionally distort the image of the Adamic civilization, as this was essential for the conspiracy to remain effective.

In other words, when an occurrence such as the war on drugs, the welfare system, or even slavery is mentioned with conspiracy, in many cases, it is usually met with pooh-poohing. Since the word conspiracy is also associated with The Power to Define, subsequently, the misrepresentation of the Black man's image will always be the center of ridicule. However, as more evidence of deception arises and becomes challenged, the Black male and his image would have to undergo a definite retrial.

Picture the structure of a seesaw; now envision the African male on the lower end and the Euro gentile on the upper end. When properly used, as the weight shifts, one end

---

[*] American Webster Dictionary.

goes up, and the other comes down. So why hasn't the African in America concluded this simple fix? The function of a seesaw is all too simple; even a child could use it correctly, but the African male has yet to discover the simplicity of its function. Now, one can understand why the Euro gentile sits so boldly and imprudently. He knows that the mind of the Africans in America has undergone a surgical brain procedure, for he's solely responsible for his new brain replacement. When the Black male realizes all he has to do is get up, then, by nature, the Euro gentile will naturally fall. For he didn't come into power because he was a great being. As the Adamic civilization descended, the Euro gentile ascended, and by nature, as the Adamic civilization ascends, unavoidably will the Euro gentile descend.

Another way to guarantee the effectiveness of a conspiracy is every member's unwavering commitment to a unique purpose. For instance, members of the FDA have approved oxycodone as a treatment for moderate to severe pain. Side effects such as dizziness, vomiting, fatigue and many more are listed, yet addiction is not mentioned as a side effect, although narcotics have been shown to have relevant forms of addiction. The conspiracy was agreed as addiction being self-inflicted even if taking the narcotic as prescribed. Let's say if this were to be true, the dosage of oxycodone began at 5mg and exceeded an outrageous dosage of 120mg-slow-release tablets, with little to no pushback whatsoever. With a 120mg tablet, addiction is the least of one's worries, death has now become predetermined.

The festering wounds of slavery are often considered the same for those who were addicted to oxycodone, self-inflicting. What's the logical outcome of introducing a 120 mg narcotic to combat chronic pain or a foolproof method designed to generate hate within the African male species? Would not the obvious outcome be addiction/death or Black-on-Black violence? "Those who have ears to hear, let them hear".

It's indisputable the harmony it took to bring about and execute what's called "The Making of a Slave." Loyalty had to be the key element, not just amid Willie Lynch and company, but even wives and children were taught never to miss an opportunity. Can you imagine a White kid, 8 years of age perhaps, being taught the art of deception? Learning to masterfully use the tactics of his father, his grandfather, and their co-conspirators' friends to keep a people envious and distrustful of one another? It should seriously cause you to consider what's actually being discussed or taught in the homes of European children regarding people of color. I can tell you what is not being discussed or taught in the homes of most Black children: the essential knowledge of God, self, history before the shores of the West, language, culture, etc.

Growing up as a man of African descent, raised by a mother of African descent, going to school and having friends of similar backgrounds, I can attest that there were little to no discussions enlightening the true history of being so-called "Black." What was taught at home, in school, and in church was heavily dominated by narratives tethered to slavery. It often felt as though our parents, teachers, and pastors were either unaware or truly did not care to know our true identity. Either of which calls into question the fundamental understanding of Blacks worshipping a Euro-centric figure as the Savior for African people.

Despite the obvious bloodshed of the African people at the hands of a common enemy, the Euro gentile triumphantly brainwashed the African species to love, respect, and trust only them.

It was necessary to assure the taskmaster that distrust is stronger than trust, envy is stronger than adulation, respect, and admiration. This simple little list of differences was significantly greater than just a little list. It was an ingenious finding of the slaveholders to study the human nature of African slaves in particular. It served as keys for control, to create and perpetuate hate, envy, and distrust.

In all actuality, the ill feelings of hate, distrust, and resentment didn't occur overnight or in a matter of weeks. The projected effect would take one year when used intensely and at every opportunity. Regardless of how small or seemingly insignificant it may be, every opportunity is every opportunity. It also implies not just passively waiting for an opportunity to arise but deliberately looking for potential opportunities to act.

After an intense indoctrination, the Black male would become self-generating, meaning he is now qualified to hate, distrust, envy, and eventually cause physical harm to his fellow man without any external pressure. He has been groomed to hate anything that looks like him (whether he's aware of it or not). I don't say it with joy; he hates himself and anything that reminds him of his African roots. He's delighted in flying within the boundaries of the U.S. If he's a celebrity of some sort, he may happily visit, but certainly, he's not giving up "the good life" in return to the motherland.

Does the relentless pursuit of material wealth in European society lead the African male to disregard the Euro-gentile as a threat to his very existence? Or is the threat only applicable or overlooked by those who have been defined as rich or poor? One cannot be naive enough to think slaves were repeatedly told to hate and distrust one another throughout an intense year. As the plan of action was instituted, along with it came inequity and favoritism among the slaves. Does the term "house nigger" and "field nigger" sound familiar? It's sourced from the favorable treatment based on the simple little list of differences.

I'm reminded of the descriptive difference between a *"house negro" and a "field negro," given by Malcolm X on the 23rd of January at Michigan State University in 1963.* Its details serve as a reference for how this trust with the master and distrust among the slaves manifested.

"So you have two types of Negro: the old type and the new type. Most of you know the old type. When you read about him in history during slavery, he was called "Uncle Tom." He was the house Negro. And during slavery, you had two Negroes. You had the house Negro and the field Negro.

The house Negro usually lived close to his master. He dressed like his master. He wore his master's second-hand clothes. He ate food that his master left on the table. And he lived in his master's house--probably in the basement or the attic--but he still lived in the master's house.

So whenever that house Negro identified himself, he always identified himself in the same sense that his master identified himself. When his master said, "We have good food," the house Negro would say, "Yes, we have plenty of good food." When the master said that "we have a fine home here," the house Negro said, "Yes, we have a fine home here." When the master was sick, the house Negro identified himself so much with his master he'd say, "What's the matter boss, we sick?" His master's pain was his pain. And it hurt him more for his master to be sick than for him to be sick himself. When the house started burning down, that type of

Negro would fight harder to put the master's house out than the master himself would.

But then you had another Negro out in the field. The house Negro was in the minority. The masses--the field Negroes were the masses. They were in the majority. When the master got sick, they prayed that he'd die. If his house caught on fire, they'd pray for a wind to come along and fan the breeze.

If someone came to the house Negro and said, "Let's go, let's separate," naturally that Uncle Tom would say, "Go where?" What could I do without a boss? Where would I live? How would I dress? Who would look out for me? That's the house Negro. But if you went to the field Negro and said, "Let's go, let's separate," he wouldn't even ask you where or how. He'd say, "Yes, let's go."*

Another great leader to represent the African people exposed too the efficacy of this foolproof method: the inability to discipline, respect, and uphold his responsibilities as a man and for brotherhood.

"The Negro in Western civilization, because of his environments that force upon him an inferiority complex, is the most stubborn individual to discipline within his own race. He has but little, if any, respect for internal racial authority. He cannot be depended upon to carry out an order given by a superior of his own race. If the superior attempts, in his presence, to enforce the order, he is undermined and assured of putting on airs. If the order is entrusted to a lieutenant, he, in turn, changes the order to suit himself and endeavors to constitute himself the superior individual. In my experience as head of the largest negro organization in the

---

* Transcribed text from the audio excerpt.

world, I have found that to every hundred orders given to be executed for the absolute good of the organization and the race, not two percent of them have been carried out in their entirety. This lack of obedience to orders and discipline checkmates the real worthwhile progress of the race. This accounts for the Negro's lack of a racial, nationalistic ideal. The only cure for him is his removal to an atmosphere entirely his own, where he would be forced, under rigid civil and other discipline, to respect himself and his own racial authority".

The Honorable Marcus M. Garvey

As men, we must first set our emotions aside and hear the substance of what's being brought forth, whether it is to expose or to mend. Anytime leadership seeks to be established in the midst of the African male, it always reverts back to the question, How come he gets to lead? The majority of African men, because of their mental incapacity, will never be qualified to lead, let alone understand leadership. Unless he rids himself completely of such indoctrination, he'll never have harmony amongst his brethren.

Curiously, the concept of a leader or king came into existence as the Children of Israel pleaded to mirror the surrounding nations. Take Samuel, for instance, who was displeased with the request of Israel to appoint them a King. When Samuel prayed to God expressing his discontent, the Creator responded thus. "Listen to all that the people are saying to you; it is not you they have rejected, but they have rejected me as their king. 8 As they have done from the day I brought them up out of Egypt until this day, forsaking me and serving other gods, so they are doing to you."

As God instructed Samuel to convey to the Children of Israel what the King who would reign over them would claim as his rights, blinded by their stubbornness, they insisted on a King anyway, but God had been their King all along. The Creator also warned them that the day will come when they will cry out to be delivered from the hands of the King they begged for and he will not answer them (**1st Samuel Chapter 8**).

Breaking the chains of psychological slavery bound by a false sense of security is perhaps the most challenging endeavor if the African male is ever to reunite. The Euro gentile will never free him from this envy and distrust, for the Black male is a recipient of his hateful doctrine. To reverse the state of his mind, he should first put aside the malicious, foolproof method. It simply creates a reversed effect of his envy and distrust toward his fellow man. The Black male does not have to emulate 400 years of slavery to heal from his diseased mind. However, he must come to the realization that, no matter where he resides on the planet, there is only one shared common oppressor.

In fact, the first largest gathering of an Afro-Asian conference took place on the 18–24th April 1955 in Bandung, West Java, Indonesia. These were nations of colored people from various religious sectors, uniting over a common cause. There were a total of twenty-nine countries that participated, representing a total population of 1.5 billion people or, at that time, approximately 54% of the world's population. The conference's stated aims were to advance Afro-Asian economic and cultural concord and to oppose colonialism or neocolonialism by any nation. Afro-

Asian leaders came to the realization they all shared one thing alike: a common oppressor. Whether the members were from West Africa being colonized by the French, East Africa being colonized by the British, the Congo colonized at the hands of Belgium, or Angola at the hands of the Portuguese, they were all being oppressed by the Euro gentile nations.

The Million Man March is also recorded as the largest gathering of colored men from across the United States converging in Washington, D.C. Similar to the Bandung Conference, prominent members of the African American communities were called to convey to the world a vastly different picture of the Black male and to unite in self-help and self-defense against the economic and social ills plaguing the African American community. The gathering was held on the 16th of October 1995 by Minister Louis Farrakhan.

Within two decades, Minister Louis Farrakhan held a "Justice or Else" rally on the 10th of October 2015, commemorating the 20th anniversary of the Million Man March. With the same issues of economics and social ills back on the table, millions of African Americans took to the streets near downtown D.C. in search of political aid. Not only was I a part of it, but I bore witness to approximately one million Black men, along with some women and children, joining under the banner of unity. Peace, however, became obsolete, Hinch "Justice or Else." Although I considered it to be an extraordinary moment, my solution to the issues that plagued us was a lot different than those I came to be surrounded by.

Some months prior to converging at the Million Man March, I flew to Israel in May, partaking in what is known to the African Hebrew Israelites of Jerusalem as "New World Passover." It's a celebration of independence commemorating the history of the Africans in America and a Sign of the times.* At the time of my arrival, Ben Ammi, the spiritual leader of the African Hebrews, had transitioned in December 2014. His decision (a vision from the angel Gabriel in 1966) to leave America in the year 1967 and convince others to do the same influenced my position some months later at the Million Man March. The two weeks I spent traveling throughout the state of Israel are beyond what words can express. The truth is, I was physically and spiritually in a much safer environment in the midst of the African Hebrews than in any ghetto in America I've lounged in. It served as proof that the African in America can truly dwell in peace and unity and blossom once he first makes peace with his Maker (Isaiah 27:5-6) and, secondly, separate himself from the very source that keeps him in chaos and confusion.

> *"And secondly, when man begins to transform his character to please the Creator, it also makes his enemies be at peace with him."*
>
> — Proverbs 6:7

Upon my return from Israel, I was finishing up a carpentry trade, which led me to take construction classes at Cincinnati State. A community college in the city of Cincinnati, Ohio. There, I bonded with a few brothers and staff. They were a part of a brotherhood program, and It was then I learned about the 20th anniversary of the Million Man March. As I shared my recent experience in Israel with one of the brothers, I could tell it had moved him. The drive from

---

* See Notes to Our Reader, Sign of the Times (**Daniel 2:44**).

Cincinnati, Ohio, to Baltimore, Maryland, where we had rented rooms and slept, lasted approximately 10 hours. On the day of the march, he and I made signs of an Exodus as we paraded alongside an estimated one million African men, some women, and children. While their signs wrote "Justice or Else, "Black lives matter," "Pro black doesn't mean Anti white" etc. Our signs were directly aimed at the President of the United States.

It read, "Mr. President, **Exodus 4:22-23** "And thou shalt say unto Pharaoh: Thus saith the LORD: Israel is My son, My first-born. And I have said unto thee: Let My son go, that he may serve Me".

From the pivotal Bandung Conference in 1955 to the reflective 20th anniversary of the Million Man March in 2015, the African proved to himself as well as the Euro-gentile that he could come together in unity and peace. He also identified the Euro-gentile as the primary contributor to his economic and social woes. Yet, he still sits on the lower end of the seesaw, neglecting or simply refusing to understand its basic function.

Written within the pages of history, the African in America has indeed shown his ability to manage and govern his own affairs. The presence and aid of the Eurogentile in the affairs of African men are a major destabilizer. In every attempt to better his position, he never changed the very thing detrimental to his existence: his oppressor. He fights for a country that doesn't fight for him on his home front. He marched, marched again, and obtained high office and higher pay, but strangely, he never considered changing masters. How could he possibly ponder such a thing when he thinks like the house negro, "Where can I find a better anything other than America?" I can say with certainty that life for the African American in the land of his ancestors is long overdue.

During the 28 days of February, more commonly known as "Black History Month," its literal objective each year is to continue to impose a set of beliefs on the Africans in America uncritically, all while giving a false sense of freedom. It serves as a constant reminder of the brutal atrocities faced at the hands of the Euro gentile. Images and videos of physical abuse are always on display. Heroic figures such as Harriet Tubman and Frederick Douglass are always seen as inspirations to overcome the physical and mental abuse of the oppressor. However, figures like Nat Turner are never put on display as inspirations to never accept such treatment. If my point is far-fetched, then let's examine this fact: biblical history proves the existence of the Adamic civilization dating back to the Genesis creation, approximately 6,000 years ago. Quite contrary to the 28 days of Black History Month, which relates only to 400 years of history since the creation of Adam.

Again, who's benefiting from suppressing this magnitude of information from the Africans in America? What does it truly signify for the Euro gentile if the Africans in America were to regain possession of their long-lost history? Remember, the objective was not only to reverse the roles of man and woman but to perpetually create a state of dependency in Black males, which has been one of his downfalls, the inability to use his God-given mind. However, with his "new mind," he must eradicate the idea that he can be in opposition to God and live. His new mind must incessantly be filled with truth and righteousness. His weakened state must be fortified with an exemplary production of strength. He must absolutely be responsible for the need for an olive branch and reconciliation with his God. Put aside the simple little list of differences; regain your definite and respectable place on this planet. No other time holds more meaning than the present.

Chapter 5
To Subdue: Of the Genesis

There undoubtedly has to be a re-educating and, ultimately, a redefining of words cunningly used to oppress and oppose. Allow me to arouse your memory briefly by returning to the pages of the book of Genesis. As the woman encounters an individual with an opposing spirit, divine guidance has already been imparted. His intentions to challenge God directly and to suppress His creation become widely clear in the manner in which he approaches the woman.

> 3 And he said unto the woman, Yea, hath God said: Ye shall not eat of any tree of the garden? 4 And the serpent said unto the woman, 'Ye shall not surely die; 5 For God doth know that in the day ye eat thereof, then your eyes shall be opened, and ye shall be as God, knowing good and evil."

> — Genesis 3:1, 4, 5

A distinct difference between education and indoctrination is critical thinking. Because African men and women lack the ability to discern between good and evil, they have only been indoctrinated and not educated. Can one obtain higher education if God is not at the core? Should a doctor who is highly educated (trained) receive a higher wage than a doctor who is Divinely educated?

It would be inept to think one can live and remain in opposition to the Creator: "In the day thou eatest thereof, thou shalt surely die." What's even more baffling is the individual who promulgates this teaching, although the instructions given were transparent. When the Bible is studied and viewed correctly from its original Hebraic thought, the prophets leave no room for error. If we remove and replace the serpentine beast of Genesis with an actual person and their actions to oppose God, then the spirit and objective of the Euro-gentile become prima facie. Enveloped in the ideology of the Euro-gentile, the Africans in America remain entirely subdued and in opposition to the Creator.

When the African in America properly aligns to re-educate and redefine the narratives and words that have long been rooted in deception, truth must become their new master. Before one could be educated, there first had to be one dedicated and devoted to the pursuit of truth in the midst of much opposition; hence, "And the LORD God commanded the man, saying: 'Of every tree of the garden thou mayest freely eat, but of the tree of the knowledge of good and evil, thou shalt not eat of it".The tree of knowledge of good and evil denotes an individual with a deviant, mutant form of intellect. It appears to be something desired, but in God's supreme wisdom, a forewarning was given to the contrary.

The current plight of the Africans in America is a direct manifestation of an evil ideology that opposes their very being. In this deviant and mutated intellect, the Spirit of Err understands the connection between the Creator and His creation—the Adamic civilization—far beyond their grasp. Accredited with the authority of God, they were entrusted with the sacred mandate to subdue the earth and exercise dominion over all living creatures, as written.

What the African man and woman lost due to their lack of obedience, the adversary gained. As they forfeited access to the Tree of Life and Power to Define ("and whatsoever the man would call every living creature, that was to be the name thereof"), he presumptuously prevailed, wrangling complete submission and dominion over the earth and its inhabitants. *The power that was invested by God into the hands of man had been invested into the hands of our enemies.* Everything existing under their control suffers (in the day thou eatest thereof thou shalt surely die"). Death, in its biblical primary meaning, was not the traditional burial; it was related to how you think and your actions. (After taking from his woman, Adam lived a total of 930 years - **Genesis 5:5**).

If one were going to oppose God, actively disagree or resist, then automatically, there would have to be another form of perception. Furthermore, this secondary perception would have to be none other than the devil or satan. For example, education is the process of "developing a mind" but who's mind? With two forms of perception, one mind would have to be of God and the other of the devil or Satan. The devil can only "develop" a mind contrary to the Creator. If the African male and female had been educated, then the question would be by who's mind, God's or the devil's?

Education was literally a form of dedication, being devoted to God's will and plan while having God at the center.

On the other hand, education in the institutions of the Euro gentile allows the worship of the devil freely. Remember, prayer was legislated out of schools, deemed unconstitutional and a violation of one's First Amendment. So again, I ask, who's responsible for developing the minds of the Africans in America?*

If prayer was deemed unconstitutional and therefore legislated out of schools, then who made the worship of the devil constitutional? (Freedom of religion) Satan cannot oppose himself; neither can God endorse an institution that will even allow the worship of opposition.

As we continue to grasp our understanding from "To Submit" to "to Subdue" under the authority of deception, it is only befitting to provide some further clarity relating to the presence and role of the Africans in Genesis. In order to duly provide the keys necessary to aid in re-educating the African species, a reimagining is strongly required.

The reconstructed narratives, lost and stolen legacies, and persistent errors in interpretation and falsifications have undeniably placed the Euro-gentile as the primary character of the Bible and the central figure of Africa. If the origins of life were in a place called Africa or Eden, then the original occupant of this place would have to be African/Edenic.

In archaeology, radiocarbon dating, or Carbon-14, is a scientific method that can accurately determine the age of organic materials as old as approximately 60,000 years. Invented in the late 1940s by Willard Libby, the importance of radiocarbon dating was summed up by Colin Renfrew

---

* *See notes to our reader, Spiritual Magna Carta.

using these exact words: Archaeology has the ability to open unimaginable vistas of thousands, even millions, of years of past human experience.

What is it about the Africans born in America that no one seems to know who we are? No prior culture, language, God, or country of origin, just 400 years of slavery. Surely, with this profound scientific method, they can discover the accurate origin of the Africans born in America beyond the shores of Africa.

In every birthplace is an undeniable truth: a birth must have occurred. In this birth or creation, the power to tame the earth and claim dominion over all living things was given to the African/Edenic male and female (**Genesis 1:26-28**).

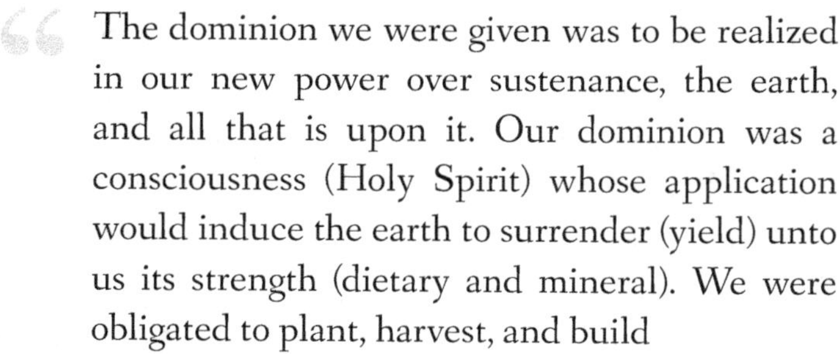

> The dominion we were given was to be realized in our new power over sustenance, the earth, and all that is upon it. Our dominion was a consciousness (Holy Spirit) whose application would induce the earth to surrender (yield) unto us its strength (dietary and mineral). We were obligated to plant, harvest, and build
>
> — The Revival of the Holy Spirit p.34, by Ben Ammi.

Man was given the understanding of how to properly relate to and harmonize with the creation from which he was made. With the innate capacity of the Divine Mind, man would preserve rather than destroy the substance of his physical creation. From the beginning, man's role was to act as the steward, nurturer, and guardian of creation, embodying a relationship that was pleasing to the Creator. Man was the presence of God on Earth.

As long as man continued in harmony with his father, he remained in harmony with creation (his mother), and creation (his fellow creatures: the fowl, the fish, and the beasts of the field) was in harmony with man and itself.

What's considered today as a natural phenomenon, such as storms, earthquakes, catastrophes, wars, animals eating animals, sickness, death, and disease, is, in actuality, unnatural and outside the realms of the intellect of God. Only through diligent study do we find these so-called natural phenomena didn't occur until after the fall of man. In addition, during the days of Noah, the rains had not fallen yet; it came up as a mist from the earth.

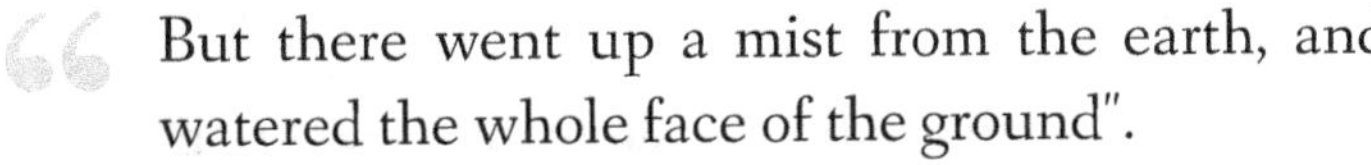

> But there went up a mist from the earth, and watered the whole face of the ground".

> — Genesis 2:6

The first usage we find of the word "submit" or to submit was actually subdue or to subdue. It related to securing and bringing everything in creation under the control or dominion of Adam. To subdue is simply the application of understanding how to utilize and constrain everything within its natural boundaries. All persons and things would show forth the effects of being governed by the spirit of God...the force behind nature, the natural.*

Keep in mind that the objective of the adversary or opposing force of Genesis was not only to cause a falling

---

* The Revival of the Holy Spirit, by Ben Ammi, p. 34

away of the Adamic civilization from their God but, upon being successful, would inherit the power invested in man by God.

Oppressed under the rule or authority of the Spirit of Err, man, woman, and Mother Earth would find themselves completely in submission or subdued. Being subjected to a condition, treatment, or operation by a spirit that was/is unwilling to subordinate itself to the Creator not only compelled the Adamic civilization to pursue a self-destructive lifestyle but also endangered the state of the planet through various methods of greed.

It is apparent that the divine design of man and woman was never intended to be in accord with this unnatural, opposing force. What would be the benefit of opposing God, the natural order, and the traditional roles of man and woman?

We find in Isaiah the brash statement made by the Spirit of Err, revealing its main objective.

> "I will ascend above the heights of the clouds; I will be like the Most High."

> — Isaiah 14:14

It's logical to conclude that the only rational explanation for opposing or going against God is the objective to kill you.

Procreation, or the producing of offspring, is a constitutive process of the Genesis creation. It's not difficult to comprehend that, in the final analysis, a reversed role in society would be detrimental, and unavoidably, the inhabitants would die off. The instructions were clear: "And in the day thou eatest thereof thou shalt surely die." Anyone taking from, consuming, or listening to that tree will certainly encounter death. Understanding, that those who take from, consume, or listen to all the other trees were promised to experience everlasting life.

The reeducation and redefining of words emanate from what is defined as "spiritual warfare," warring against universally accepted lies and predetermined definitions. The war, or confrontation, between the Sons of Light (prophetically known as the Children of Israel) and the Sons of Darkness* (Satan and his angels), sets the stage for the reeducation (rededication) and redefining process.

In the Book of **Revelation, chapter 12, verses 7-9**, the author gives an abstract account of where this spiritual warfare will take place and the end result of casting down deception. I will provide an exegesis following the 9th verse.

> 7 And there was a war in heaven: Michael and his angels fought against the dragon, and the dragon fought and his angels. 8. And prevailed not; neither was their place found any more in heaven. 9. And the great dragon was cast out, that old serpent called the Devil, and Satan, which deceiveth the whole world; he was cast out into the earth, and his angels were cast out with him."

---

* *See notes to reader Spiritual Warfare. And Messianic Glossary p 177
**See notes to the reader: Heaven.

Exegesis:

 And there was a confrontation between Truth and deception in the minds of the people. One like God (Yah-H-Wah), or the anointed, and his army fought an evil governing system and its army or advocates.

And this evil army of principles was not able to maintain its presence in the minds of the annoyed people anymore.

And the great evil spirit, spiritually representing the serpent in the Garden of Eden, was purged out of the minds of the anointed people that oppose the adversary of God (Yah-H-Wah), Satan, who deceiveth the whole world, who found habitations in the institutions of humanity, and his messengers/advocates were revealed and cast out with him."

— Conceptualizing The Holy Scriptures From Hebraic Thought: A Hermeneutic and Exegesis Study of the Hebrew Cannon by Sar Elyakeem Ben Yehuda, pp. 80-81

The war in heaven, or the mind, is the confrontation between Truth, one who is like God and his army, and deception, an evil governing system and his army. (Consider "Uncle Sam," a figure of the United States government and an embodiment of the country). What we once took as a single individual was actually a representation of the U.S. This system of deception did not prevail; it ceased to dwell in heaven (the highest point of one's mind).

Further on in verse 10, the author of Revelation makes it explicitly clear about the outcome

> 10 Then I heard a loud voice in heaven say: "Now have come the salvation and the power and the kingdom of our God, and the authority of His Messiah".

We must not overlook the crucial fact that deception is the foremost cause of the diminishing strength among the masses of this world. As the African in America continues to hold fast to deceit, they render themselves oblivious to the very salvation destined for them. It is only by confronting and casting aside these deceptions that truth can take root within the consciousness, allowing the Adamic civilization to truly embrace the reality of a promised deliverance and the imminent Kingdom of God on Earth.

Remember, deception is the very tool that has been used to convince the people that the Kingdom of God would be off in some remote place above the clouds. The Garden of Eden, prior to deception (the encounter with the serpent), was the only heaven that man and woman ever knew. There was no abode beyond the clouds. The Garden of Eden represented the pristine state of cognitive perfection or heaven.

It is evident how the devil has deceived the whole world. Satan has been successful in his craftiness by causing man to disassociate his job, business, eating habits, shopping habits, and recreational pastimes from the worship of God. Only when we understand how cultural expressions determine worship will we totally comprehend how to build and live in a world where all people love and worship God. Since the greatest obstacle preventing our reconciliation with God is Satan, it stands to reason that we must recognize the characters and culture that revealed Satan's presence. (Resurrection From Judgement to Post-judgement p. 196)

> Now it shall come to pass, if you diligently obey the voice of the Lord your God, to observe carefully all His commandments which I command you today, that the Lord your God will set you high above all nations of the earth. And all these blessings shall come upon you and overtake you because you obey the voice of the Lord your God."

— Deuteronomy 28: 1-15

These books can be found on Amazon